Blueprints: Rebuilding Lives and Redesigning Futures

Bull City YouthBuild

Durham, North Carolina

spi
STUDENT PRESS INITIATIVE

2017

Blueprints: Rebuilding Lives and Redesigning Futures
A Collection of Essays and Poems from Bull City YouthBuild Students

SPI Site Educator:
Crystal Chen Lee

Triangle Literacy Council CEO: Laura Walters
Triangle Literacy Council Senior Director: Kristen Corbell
Bull City YouthBuild Program Director: Cory Rawlinson
Bull City YouthBuild Construction Instructor: Joe Hall

Director, SPI: Roberta Lenger Kang
Initiative Leader, SPI: Cristina Compton
Founding Director, SPI: Erick Gordon
Director and Founder, CPET: Ruth Vinz
Cover Design: Kapo Amos Ng
Interior Layout: Crystal Chen Lee
Photographs: YouthBuild Site Teachers and Coordinators

Student Press Initiative (SPI), Box 182
The Center for the Professional Education of Teachers
Teachers College, Columbia University
525 West 120th Street
New York, NY 10027
www.tc.cpet/edu

DEDICATION

This book is dedicated to YouthBuild students across the country and their networks of support who encourage them in their endeavors.

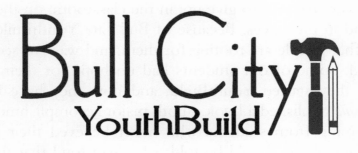

FOREWORD

A little over a year ago, I was sitting in my office at the Triangle Literacy Council when I received a call notifying me that our organization was lucky enough to receive a grant from the United States Department of Labor to start a YouthBuild program in East Durham. We set off on the daunting task of launching a program that would help young adults, ages 16 to 24, earn their high school diplomas while learning construction skills through building affordable housing for low-income people in their neighborhood.

We hired staff and recruited students, and named the program "Bull City YouthBuild" after a local nickname for Durham. But Bull City YouthBuild became so much more for everyone involved than just an educational program. It became a family, and a place of hope. Students inspire each other every day not to give up: in the classroom, on the work site, and in their lives. Because of Bull City YouthBuild, they know that people are rooting for them, and want to see them succeed. Some of our students had no hope for their future before they started YouthBuild, and now they have built a house *and* published a book – both major accomplishments!

Coming from students who never believed their stories were valuable or should be told, I am so proud that they are able to share their stories with you. In their own words, you will hear about their experiences growing up, what it's like to finally achieve a high school diploma, what Bull City YouthBuild means to them, and so much more. I invite you to take a journey with them through the following pages, to a place where rebuilding lives and redesigning futures is possible.

Laura Walters
President and CEO, Triangle Literacy Council

ACKNOWLEDGEMENTS

This book would not be possible without the foundation of the YouthBuild authors and their teachers. Their stories and their voices are just a glimpse of their incredible journey in Bull City YouthBuild.

I want to thank the Triangle Literacy Council for their partnership and for their human and financial resources in thie project. I specifically name Laura Walters, Cory Rawlinson, and Joe Hall for their tireless efforts and encouragements in pushing this project forward. I especially want to thank Dr. Kristen Corbell for being the site coordinator and for making sure the publication is a manifestation of the students' stories.

I also thank North Carolina State University for its generous funding and its contribution to seek and meet the needs of historically underserved populations in North Carolina. Because of the College of Education's mission and vision to reach the community, this publication can be distributed to even more leaders and educators.

Last but not least, thank you to the Student Press Initiative staff and Dr. Cristina Compton for their partnership in this project. Their continued dedication in pursuing social justice is always an inspiration to witness.

It is with great honor and immense gratitude that we present this book as the inaugural Bull City YouthBuild publication---we hope it is just the beginning blueprint of more young voices to come.

Dr. Crystal Chen Lee
Assistant Professor, North Carolina State University
Student Press Initiative Educator

ACKNOWLEDGEMENTS

NC STATE UNIVERSITY

The Blueprints project is an outstanding example of the type of work we do and the type of partnerships we form in the NC State College of Education to live out our land-grant mission to engage communities where they are in order to address the needs of all learners, especially those in underserved communities. I'm inspired by the extraordinary leadership, relationship-building, and commitment to social justice that Dr. Crystal Lee and her colleagues have demonstrated in making the Blueprints project a reality. The students' essays exemplify the power of community literacy and why our faculty members' work in the field is critical to the well-being of North Carolina.

Mary Ann Danowitz. D.Ed.
Dean, College of Education
North Carolina State University

ACKNOWLEDGEMENTS

NC STATE UNIVERSITY

In the Department of Teacher Education and Learning Sciences in the College of Education at North Carolina State University, we prepare professionals who are committed to equity and social justice. In fulfilling this mission, our faculty work with community-based organizations to meet the needs of currently underserved populations. The Blueprints project is a wonderful example of a community and university partnership aimed at providing students with opportunities to succeed in school and life. Kudos to Dr. Crystal Chen Lee and her colleagues on this transformational project.

Dr. John Lee
Department Head and Professor
Teacher Education and Learning Sciences
North Carolina State University

NC STATE UNIVERSITY

TABLE OF CONTENTS

III. Where I'm From: A Poem of Our Foundations

IV. Why Youthbuild? – A Persuasive Essay on Constructing a Blueprint

V. Building a House Together- Following the Blueprints for a Home

VI. We are BullCity YouthBuild : A Collective Blueprint and Collaborative Poem

About the Authors

Appendix

*Pseudonym used

INTRODUCTION

Dr. Crystal Chen Lee
Assistant Professor, North Carolina State University

In September 2017, I stepped foot into the Triangle Literacy Council office hoping to embark on a budding writing project: to have students publish a book that highlighted the work of the Durham community. As the conversation with Laura Walters and Kristen Corbell grew, I found that the work of the community was strong, and what was even more powerful was the work of its teachers and students. The work, specifically the voices of Bull City YouthBuild, had to be shared and heard.

Now, as we close out the year in December 2017, we are incredibly encouraged by not only the work that YouthBuild students have accomplished—their attainment of a high school diploma, the achievement of building an entire house, but here, the publication of their very own book in a matter of months. These authors should be celebrated and honored—for their work is not in vain; it is a testament to the way they are constructing the new blueprints of future generations.

Having worked tirelessly through these pieces every week during the fall semester, these authors speak about their past, present, and future to give our community, our schools, our educators, and our institutions an invaluable gift: the initial wonderings of how we may best meet the needs of students in North Carolina. Let them educate us here---for their words are truth and their stories speak to the narrative of how communities, schools, and institutions can work together for equity.

About the Educator:

Dr. Crystal Chen Lee

Dr. Crystal Chen Lee is an Assistant Professor of English Language Arts and Literacy in the College of Education at North Carolina State University. Her research lies at the nexus of literacy, historically underserved youth, and community organizations. One of her greatest passions is empowering students to have their voices known through reading, writing, and speaking. As a former Student Press Initiative Educator in New York City, she is very excited about this inaugural project with Bull City YouthBuild, and is consistently encouraged by the writers of *Blueprints: Rebuilding Lives and Redesigning Futures*. Dr. Lee began her teaching experience as a high school English teacher in New Jersey. She received her Ed.D. in Curriculum and Teaching from Columbia University.

INTRODUCTION

Dr. Kristen Corbell
Triangle Literacy Council
Senior Program Director of Curriculum and Accountability

I began working with Bull City YouthBuild in August 2017 when I was hired as the Senior Director of Curriculum and Program Accountability of Triangle Literacy Council. I have spent many hours working with our YouthBuild students and soon-to-be graduates as they have written this book and prepared for taking HiSET tests to earn their High School Equivalency diploma. In the short amount of time of teaching the students, I saw students actively engaged and pushing themselves to tackle even the hardest problems and unwilling to give up. These are skills they will take with them the rest of their lives. I am so proud of what they have learned and accomplished.

The book was a way to have our students learn how to write in an effective formal manner, but also have a product of their hard work for which they can be proud. The writing skills learned would first help the students on the High School Equivalency test, but more importantly it will help them learn writing skills they can use both in post-secondary education and their chosen careers. The students have put their heart and soul into these pieces, and I look forward to seeing their faces at graduation as they read their books to their family and friends.

About the Educator:
Dr. Kristen Corbell

Dr. Kristen Corbell is originally from South Carolina, before moving with her family to North Carolina. After graduating from Winthrop University in Rock Hill, SC with a bachelor degree in Mathematics and Secondary Education, she moved to Durham, NC and taught middle school and coordinated the math program for six years. After teaching, she attended and graduated from NC State University with a MS in Curriculum Development and Supervision and Ph.D. in Curriculum and Instruction, Educational Psychology. After graduation, Dr. Corbell worked in education program evaluation.

Since 2006, Dr. Corbell has published a book chapter and several journal articles. While working at the North Carolina Community College System, she found her professional goal of working with adult education programs to help students receive their High School Equivalency and prepare them for work and college. Dr. Corbell is currently the Senior Director of Curriculum and Program Accountability at Triangle Literacy Council where she oversees the adult education program, Bull City YouthBuild, and the Juvenile Literacy Center.

INTRODUCTION

Cory Rawlinson
Bull City YouthBuild Program Director

Stay Woke

"Some people dream of success while others wake up and work."
-Unknown

Our students have overcome situations and circumstances in which others would and have literally failed in. Our students come to us broken, distraught, upset, confused and honestly betrayed about the cards life has dealt them. Yes, we support students who have dropped out of school or who function with low literacy but they still have dreams of success. The greatest asset Bull City Youth Build provides our students is an atmosphere to wake up. To wake up from the slumber that produces laziness and bitterness. To wake up from the slumber that produces entitlement and lack of preparation. To wake up from the slumber that produces forgetfulness or passiveness. Here at BCYB we provide an atmosphere which encourages our students to wake up from this notion that dreams come to those that wait and instead, to work hard to making those dreams come true. Bull City YouthBuild is a program comprised of WOKE, intelligent, hard-working, successful young people who are ready to be the leaders of today and tomorrow. Stay WOKE BCYB. Stay WOKE.

About the Educator:

Cory Rawlinson

A mentor by call and by profession, Mr. Rawlinson has over fifteen years of experience working with at-risk youth. Cory attended North Carolina Central University where he received a Bachelor of Arts degree in English Literature and a Master's of Public Administration degree, also from North Carolina Central University. Mr. Rawlinson is serves faithfully on the ministerial staff of Grace Church of Durham. Cory Rawlinson is married to Minister Tarica Rawlinson and is the father of two, Cory and Christian.

INTRODUCTION

Joe Hall
Bull City YouthBuild Construction Instructor

I'm so proud of my students. These young people worked hard hours through a hot Durham summer. They showed up regularly and went home tired. They worked together as a team and together, they built an entire house. Along the way, they learned that they could use hand and power tools to transform their world. Now they are accomplished crafts people. They are rightfully proud of themselves. I'm very proud of them and proud to show off the house they built.

Completed Habitat for Humanity House
Constructed by
Bull City YouthBuild 2017-2018 Class

About the Educator:

Joe Hall
Bull City YouthBuild Construction Instructor

I love structures and the craft they involve you in. It seems I spent my childhood building "forts', I attended architect school at Georgia Tech. My first job was with a remodeling company where I learned every part of home building. Right after I got married, we bought a hundred year-old house for $16,000. For three years, all my spare time and money went to fix it up. We've built 5 other houses for ourselves since then and I've built hundreds of suburban-homes, cottages, McMansions, Habitat for Humanity homes and a mountain lodge. But I'm most proud of the house I worked with my students to build this year.

My Life's Blueprint: A Personal Essay on Rebuilding Lives and Redesigning Futures

Inspired by Dr. Martin Luther King Jr.'s speech entitled, "What is Your Life's Blueprint?" the authors of this book set out to draft their life's blueprint as an introduction to how they might rebuild lives and redesign futures through Bull City YouthBuild and their own future trajectories. Some were inspired to select a quote from Dr. Martin Luther King's speech to inspire their writing and drafting. This first piece sets the ground for the extended metaphor of blueprints—drawing a life's blueprint while using a house blueprint to build a home for their community.

--

Photograph by Julian Wasser, Time Life Pictures/Getty Images

"What is Your Life's Blueprint?" Transcript

On October 26, 1967, six months before he was assassinated, Dr. Martin Luther King Jr. spoke to a group of students at Barratt Junior High School in Philadelphia.

I want to ask you a question, and that is: What is your life's blueprint? This is the most important and crucial period in your lives. For what you do now and what you decide now at this age my well determine which way your life shall go.

Whenever a building is constructed, you usually have an architect who draws a blueprint, and that blueprint serves as the pattern, as the guide, and a building is not well erected without a good, sound, and solid blueprint.

Now, each of you is in the process of building the structure of your lives, and the question is whether you have a proper, a solid and a sound blueprint.

I want to suggest some of the things that should begin your life's blueprint. Number one in your life's blueprint, should be a deep belief in your own dignity, your worth and your own somebodiness. Don't allow anybody to make you feel that you're nobody. Always feel that you count. Always feel that you have worth, and always feel that your life has ultimate significance. Now that means that you should not be ashamed of your color. You know, it's very unfortunate that in so many instances, our society has placed a stigma on the Negro's color.

Secondly, in your life's blueprint you must have as the basic principle the determination to achieve excellence in your various fields of endeavor. You're going to be deciding as the days, as the years unfold what you will do in life — what your life's work will be. Once you have decided what it will be, set out to do it, and to do it well.

And I say to you, my young friends, doors are opening to you--doors of opportunities that were not open to your mothers and your fathers — and the great challenge facing you is to be ready to face these doors as they open.

Ralph Waldo Emerson, the great essayist, said in a lecture in 1871, "If a man can write a better book or preach a better sermon or make a better mousetrap than his neighbor, even if he builds his house in the woods, the world will make a beaten path to his door."

This hasn't always been true — but it will become increasingly true, and so I would urge you to study hard, to burn the midnight oil; I would say to you, don't drop out of school. I understand all the sociological reasons, but I urge you that in spite of your economic plight, in spite of the situation that you're forced to live in — stay in school.

And when you discover what you going to be in your life, set out to do it as if God Almighty called you at this particular moment in history to do it. Do that job so well that the living, that the living, the dead, or the unborn couldn't do it any better.

If it falls your lot to be a street sweeper, sweep streets like Michelangelo painted pictures, sweep streets like Beethoven composed music. Sweep streets like Shakespeare wrote poetry. Sweep streets so well that all the hosts of heaven and earth will have to pause and say: Here lived a great street sweeper who swept his job well.

If you can't be a pine at the top of the hill, be a shrub in the valley. Be the best little shrub on the side of the hill. For it isn't by size that you win or you fail. Be the best of whatever you are.

Finally, in your life's blueprint, there must be a commitment to the eternal principles of beauty, love, and justice. Don't allow anybody to pull you so low as to make you hate them. Don't allow anybody to cause you to lose your self-respect to the point that you do not struggle for justice. However young you are, you have a responsibility to see to make life better for everybody. And so, you must be involved in the struggle for freedom and justice.

-Dr. Martin Luther King Jr.

My Life's Blueprint: New Beginnings
Jane Rodriguez

I see YouthBuild as a start to a new path. Bull City YouthBuild is a foundation for me to become independent. To me, independence means to be disciplined and responsible. In order to be disciplined and responsible, I need to have clear goals for myself.

My first goal is to graduate from high school and get my diploma. YouthBuild is helping me to receive my diploma. When I graduate, it will be my first successful accomplishment. My next goal is to find a job and find scholarships for college. I want to work while taking classes in order to pay my tuition and living expenses. I want to attend a community college in order to build my career.

My long-term goal is to become an architect. However, I need to work to get there. Therefore, my first attainable goal is to become a bank accountant. By studying bank accounting, I can have a secure job to achieve my long-term goal. Sometimes it may be difficult, so along the way, I want to develop some backup plans.

While pursuing my long-term goal, my mid-term goals are to educate myself on other topics such as learning about property law, financial marketing, and management. To achieve my long-term goal, I want to learn how to own property through experiencing how to start a business while budgeting the finances. By learning how to budget, I can work up to my dream career of becoming an architect and building homes. My dream is to create houses and sell them.

By setting these clear goals, I can start my new path and achieve the vision I have after graduating from Bull City YouthBuild.

My Life's Blueprint
Tat O.

"Number 1 in my life blueprint should be a deep belief in your own dignity."

Dignity means honor and respect. Respect is a big thing in my life and life itself. Having respect can get you very far in life.

My life's blueprint begins from my past to where I am now to my future. It all started when I was 3 years old and my mom passed away. From that point, my life changed forever. I had one sibling who was my older brother and my aunt took care of us. She did very well with it also.

When I was 13, my oldest brother passed away. I then entered a gang and started making bad decisions. I ended up going to jail. I picked up a few charges. My charges were a couple of gun charges. It took a big toll on my life. I'm now on probation and house arrest, and it has impacted my life in good and bad ways. Of course, I want my freedom but this restriction helps me a lot because it has kept me from getting in trouble and motivated me in a lot of positive ways.

I'm expected to graduate on 1-25-18. Once I graduate, I plan to go to college to get my business license to acquire my own barber shop. I want two or maybe three barber shops called Tee's Shop and YG & Tee's Shop. I want to own my shops but I also want to work in both of them sometimes.

Lastly, I want to be a therapist and help people with their problems. I'm a very good listener and I give great advice because I have my own story to tell.

My Life's Blueprint
Kevin Sims

Growing up was kind of hard for me. Growing up with my older sister (who is two years older than me and 27 years old) and a few cousins was hard too, because I was the smallest out of everyone. I was tossed around and bullied because I was short with a big head, etc.

In addition, going to school was the worst time of my life. I got picked on, got into fights, and got suspended. I am so happy that I graduated high school and got my diploma. If I didn't, I would have to go and get my diploma from college or I might even be dead.

Years later, after I graduated high school, I attended Lyndon B. Johnson Job Corps. I was extremely nervous from the first month to month and a half there because I didn't know anyone and it was a new environment. I spent 9.5 to 10 months there. It was a great experience because I took up Facilities Maintenance. I also got my driver's license while I was there.

Now that I have my license, my goal is to be a driver for any company. I still have some work to do on my driving skills. Even if have to beg people to let me use their car, I will do my best at whatever job I get.

In the future, I would like to help little kids to stay out of jail. To do this, I'll help them discover life skills such as getting bike parts and teaching them how to fix them up.

My Life's Blueprint
Nysheed Clinton

"That if a man can write a better book or preach a better sermon, or make a better mouse trap than his neighbor even if he builds his house in the woods, the world will make a beaten path to his door."

This quote inspired me because it reminds me that if you work hard, you can be successful. I'm willing to work as hard as I can to be successful in life because I don't want to be like the other person. I want to try to be better so I can say that I did it by myself. However, I would try to get help because I know that I can't do everything on my own.

To be successful, I have set out some goals that I would like to accomplish. Most importantly, I want to finish school so I can get a job as an Electromechanical Equipment Assembler. To get that, I need to get a high school diploma, and take the classes for the job so I know what I need to do on the job. Once I get the job, I want to be able to buy my own house, travel, and go different places. By setting these goals, I am reminded that I must work hard in order to achieve them.

The Meaning of Bull City YouthBuild: A Personal Reflection

Part of the journey in constructing a life's blueprint was being a member of Bull City YouthBuild. In a personal reflection, the authors reflect on what Bull City YouthBuild has meant to them as participants of inaugural Bull City YouthBuild class.

Bull City YouthBuild Students in the Summer of 2017

What YouthBuild Means to Me
Tat O.

I have a lot of experience with YouthBuild. From where we came from to where we are now, we have improved so much. One of my personal accomplishments with YouthBuild is being able to make great progress in my academics. For example, I took a TABE (Test of Adult Basic Education) test recently and went up two grade levels in my math. I was never a good test taker until I became a part of YouthBuild.

In the beginning of YouthBuild, we were making a lot of mistakes, but now, we have improved in so many areas. YouthBuild has made me a better person and has taught me academics and skills training that I couldn't understand at a public school--nothing went well for me there. However, now I have learned that improving these areas is a learning process and I am grateful that I had the opportunity in YouthBuild to do so.

What Does YouthBuild Mean to Me?
Jermaine Quick

What does YouthBuild Mean to Me?

What Youthbuild means to me is guiding me to the right path of success. When I think of YouthBuild, I think of young teenagers trying to build up their education by going back to school. Through completing YouthBuild, I can learn the construction trade and get OSHA (Occupational Safety and Health Administration) certified in order to secure a job. In addition, through studying in YouthBuild, I can get my high school equivalency diploma.

Bull City YouthBuild is different from school because I can get good benefits of trade and certification. You can't get a second chance at high school but you can at Bull City YouthBuild-- that's why they made the program for people who dropped out.

Bull City YouthBuild Meaning
Kevin Sims

To me, YouthBuild means that I have the opportunity to get myself on the right track. If you join YouthBuild, you start by meeting other kids who are about your age. Then, you start building on a house and give back to your community. Lastly, being in Youthbuild allows you to achieve academically.

If you join, you will get your GED or High School Equivalency Diploma. It will be one of the best programs that you will ever attend. It is either you want it or you don't.

Kevin Sims: Working on the porch in November 2017

Bull City YouthBuild Means...

Nysheed McClinton

Bull City YouthBuild means a lot to me because the program helps us get our education the way that we want to learn. It helps us give back to the community by having us build a house for a family. I like working on the house because it brings the class together to work as a team to get the job done. We can get along and work as one group.

I like the teachers because they know that everyone is different so they try to help us in ways that we understand. They try to teach us an easier way of doing things other teachers do not do. Other teachers will teach you in a way that is confusing.

They help us get a good job so we will not have to work at a place that we do not like. They help us get jobs by teaching us to master the skills we need to do well in the interview. They also teach us how to write a resume. Through their assistance, the only thing we need to do is get to our jobs on time and do whatever we need to do to keep the job.

YouthBuild is…

J'nasi Little

I AM…
BOLD
UNIQUE
LEARNER
LOYAL
CONFIDENT
INTELLIGENT
TENACIOUS
YOUTHBUILD
I AM YOUTHBUILD!!!

We're a family and will always bring a pleasing and welcoming comfort to the cohort. We won't deny or be malicious to anyone; we're eager to help the ones that need it.

Where I'm From: A Poetry Collection on the Foundation of Our Blueprints

Adapted from George Ella Lyon's poem, "Where I'm From," these authors explore the foundation of their blueprints--their past--in order to build and rebuild their futures.

I am from those moments--
snapped before I budded --
leaf-fall from the family tree.
-George Ella Lyon

Before the foundation was made for the house
"From which this house stood"

What was, What is, What will be.

Jane Rodriguez

I am from a belief in God.
From the hard-working to helping hands.
I am from "*I can do anything*".
I am from a broken home and a busy parent,
Where hands are busy through the day, and tired,
But keep going.
I am from where no one taught me what's right from
wrong,
But still living life to the *fullest*.
I am from the highs and lows and
the moments in between
From where you are now and where you'll be.

Where I'm From

I was born in a cruel and unique place
Where everybody smile and giggle in your face
And pretend they real but they really fake
That's when the cruel part starts to take place
Shooting everyday
When you walk out your door you praying you make it
back the same way
86 people killed to gun violence
The tragedy leaving him or her faced up in that casket
You can never get caught lacking
Where I'm from its called Bull City
It's a lot of fashion and people rocking fittys
Yet it's also a very progressive city
With a lot of jobs and opportunities
A lot of people motivating you to go beyond your limit

Tat O.

Where I'm From
Kevin Sims

I am from hoops and trees
I am from inside Bull City
With bums with dirty sleeves
I am from the trees and the breeze

I am from a family of two and I hoop
I am from Shannon (Mom) and Cleo (Dad)
They like to laugh, get drunk, and they start to shoot
From the Tooth fairy to Santa Clause
I was mad-- I needed food

I am from "seed time and harvest" and high praises
I'm from the city of medicine, pizza and fries
I am from a small hood in the city
And I made a lot of friends

Walking from the streets of Walltown
To the whiteboards of Riverside
I am from a smart family, good education--
An awesome basketball and football player.

Where I'm From
Nysheed McClinton

I am from the woods
From deer running across the yard
From long roads, next to trees
I am from all different animals chasing
I am from playing outside with my family and friends

I am from home cooked meals every night
From staying up all night and waking up early
I am from getting together with the family on Sundays

Where I'm From
J'Nasi Little

I'm from a city where life isn't valued
Criticism here, domestic violence there
And there's murder all around you.
You have a choice to either pick or choose
Because you don't want to get lit up like a Pikachu.

Find a route or journey that fits you
It will show you the exit you're leading to.
Durham is so small that you have no choice
But to not fall
Because nobody wants to see you stand tall.
They just want you to be the little "Durhamite" you are.

Looks and words are very deceiving
Don't listen to others' opinions
When it's your goals that you're achieving
What you believe can always be achieved.

From the beginning:
Students working together at the construction site

Why YouthBuild?: A Persuasive Essay

In preparation for the high school equivalency exam, the authors wrote a persuasive essay convincing a friend to enroll in Bull City YouthBuild. Their essays demonstrate their opinions and their reasons for the values they hold in this program. In the following section, you will see the students' prompt for the essay, and their responses to it.

BULLCITY YOUTHBUILD Persuasive Writing:

WRITING SITUATION

A 17-year-old friend, Darren, is thinking about applying to BullCity Youthbuild. He is wondering if he should get his high school diploma, or if it is worth the effort to be involved in the program. Right now, he is trying to find a job and hanging with his friends in the meantime. Mr. Cory and Ms. Kristen have asked you to write an essay explaining why it is or is not a good choice for Darren to join Bull City Youthbuild.

What is your point of view?

DIRECTIONS for WRITING TASK

Write an essay either supporting or opposing the choice to join Youthbuild. Use facts, examples, personal experience, and other evidence to support your point of view.

<u>A well-written and high-scoring essay includes:</u>

You must take a side of the argument.

1. Five paragraphs that include <u>three solid arguments of the chosen side</u>
2. <u>Thesis</u> that demonstrates the purpose of the essay
3. Arguments with clear and <u>well-developed support</u>
4. <u>Cohesive and organized construction</u>
5. Minor or no grammatical errors

YouthBuild Persuasive Essay
Kevin Sims

Bull City YouthBuild is a good program to join. You learn a lot for nine months. By joining YouthBuild, you get your OSHA certificate, get paid every two weeks, and receive your high school equivalence diploma.

First, you should join Bull City YouthBuild because the staff here will help you. There is a 10-hour OSHA course that you have to take so you know how to be safe on the site. OSHA stands for Occupational Safety and Health Administration, and receiving this certification allows you to know how to be create a safe environment for you and the workers around you. It teaches you to be aware of your surroundings and to wear safety equipment.

Second, by working at YouthBuild, you will get a stipend (money). You will get paid every two weeks; every two weeks you can get $100 dollars. In addition, you get a bonus for passing your HiSET (High School Equivalency Test) or doing a good job on the construction site. It may not be much, but it is kind of helpful if you do not have any money in your pocket.

There are five HiSET exams that you have to take to earn your High School Equivalency. You have to get eight to pass the test. Make sure you set up each test, take it, and pass it. It's as easy as pie. All you really have to do is study; the teachers will help you study by giving you practice test.

It is a nine-month program. The staff can help you figure out what you want to do if you do not already know. You have until the end of the program to find out what you want to do. When the program is over, the teachers will help you find a job to build your future career. Therefore, joining Bull City YouthBuild will allow you to gain certification, receive a high school diploma, be employed, and set you on a new path.

Why YouthBuild?

Nysheed McClinton

Dear Darren,

I think you should join Bull City YouthBuild because if you do not know what you want to do in life, coming to Bull City YouthBuild is a good plan. The program will help you find a job and get your high school diploma. The staff will even help you get a construction certificate if you ever want to work on construction. It does not take long to complete the program; it only takes 9 months to finish.

The teachers can help you get a good job so you will not have to work at a place you do not like. For example, they help us secure jobs by teaching us how to master the skills we need such as learning interview skills and writing a resume. Therefore, when you apply to the job and get accepted, all you need to do is arrive on time and make sure you can keep the job.

In addition, they prepare us to take academic tests. To teach us how to take the test, we learn different subjects two days a week. We study math, social studies and reading. When you pass all of your tests, you get your diploma. The teachers here are cool and caring; they will try everything they can to help you complete the program. They will help you get ready for your test so you are able to pass. Once you are done with your test, you can get your high school diploma.

Furthermore, the teachers will also help you learn life skills. For example, they will teach you how to keep track of time because they only let you miss four hours of program time. If you are responsible, they pay you depending on how much you come to school.

Lastly, they will help you get experience with the construction work because we all build a house together through YouthBuild. Right now, we work only two days a week on the house that we are building. Building the house is fun because you and your classmates get together to build the house for the community. Working on the house also gives you a chance to get your construction certificate, which you will need if you ever want to continue working at a construction site.

Based on my own experiences with Bull City YouthBuild, I think that you are going to like this. This is a great program for young adults who are looking forward to a successful path in life and who need help getting there. The teachers are always looking forward to helping anybody that needs it. The people in the program teach you that you can do anything you want in life if you just put your mind to it.

Sincerely,
Nysheed McClinton

Why YouthBuild?

Tat O.

Darren,

I would strongly suggest that you go to YouthBuild. Bull City YouthBuild (BCYB) has a lot to offer you in just a short amount of time. It's only a 9-month program that helps you get your high school equivalency, a construction trade, and a potential job or college career.

First, BCYB is more than just a program; it is more like a family. Your classmates will lift you up through all of your hard times. Once you get into YouthBuild, it is nothing but happiness. I can promise you-- you will not get the same love at another program or get all that can be offered in 9 months.

However, you may not like the long hours of school. At BCYB, you have to be there from 9am to 5pm. It may seem like a lot of hours but you are only there from Monday through Thursday. The long hours will pay off in the end. You cannot let the time discourage you. In addition, we also get to take trips during this time. We took a trip to Elizabeth City and while we were there, we visited another YouthBuild, visited East Carolina University, went to the beach, had a lot of fun, and even went out to eat afterwards.

I have tried many programs and did not succeed or go through with them. Yet, when I joined YouthBuild, I knew I was going to finish and here I am-- about to graduate in one month. When you have a lot of weak thoughts about finishing school, everyone at BCYC is going to motivate you to come. They do not care if they have to pick you up. Once you are enrolled in YouthBuild, it is the key to success.

Sincerely,
Tat O.

Building a House Together: Following the Blueprints of a Home

One of the YouthBuild projects was constructing a house for Habitat for Humanity. By being on site and working together as a team, the authors learned about the power of teamwork and the hard work of following a blueprint. Here, they reflect on their stories through the memories and experience of building the house as a class.

Constructing the house in the hot Durham summer of 2017

Building a House with YouthBuild
Tat O.

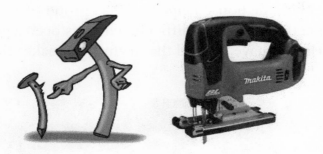

Hammering was my favorite part of building the house. I chose this memory because out of everything there is to do, I am quick to grab a hammer and a nail. Until I used a hammer, I always thought building would be very hard. Despite having an accident with the hammer, I learned the correct way to beat the nail so that I would not get hurt anymore.

Yet, I have had accidents with the hammer as well. One day, it was a hot day in the summertime and while we were building the house, I hammered my hand. Within the time of building a house, I've experienced so many different things and learned more about tools.

My second favorite tool is the jigsaw saw. I was the go-to person to use the jigsaw. If anything needed to be done, I was right there to do it. In addition, one of my hobbies is drawing, and I used that talent by painting the air vents on the front of the house. By painting the air vents, we can bring out the beauty of the house. When you first see the house, you cannot miss the painting.

During the process of building the house, we have become closer as one. We are more like a family than just classmates; building the house helped me feel proud of completing something that was difficult. This has been a great experience because I have learned that teamwork makes the dream work.

House near completion in 2017
*Painted air vents by Tat O.

Constructing a House Together:
Using Blueprints to Give Back to the Community

Nysheed McClinton

In building the house, I think about how the wood came a long way from being pieces of wood to becoming a house. When I first arrived at Bull City YouthBuild, I saw stacks of wood on the ground and ever since, we used the wood to build a house. We followed a blueprint and slowly, over time, the wood became parts of the house. The wood is the main resource of the house and as builders, we had to take care of the resource so the house would be sturdy.

When working with the wood, I was surprised that I could use some of the tools like the nail gun and the miner saw. The nail gun is a gun that shoots out nails so I did not have to waste time hammering it into the wood. The miner saw was not hard to use either; it was just that I had to get the measurements right before cutting it. Learning how to use these tools made the job more efficient.

Just like how the wood came a long way, so did our team. The farther we got on the house, the stronger our relationships became. We learned that if we work together as a team, teamwork could build friendships. When I first got here, I did not know anyone, but when we all got out to the work site, we started to work together. Over time, I started to meet a lot of new people which help start our friendships.

Finishing the house was a highlight because I can look back on the good times that I had with all of my friends. I also think the best part was the finished product because it demonstrated the hard work that we put into the house as a team. Most importantly, the house represents all the memories that I had with all of my classmates.

Constructing a House Together:
The Foundation

Kevin Sims

I chose the foundation as a significant part of the house because without a foundation, there would be no house. The house would just be floating in mud. You need a foundation and with no foundation, you will end up going nowhere in life.

In reflecting on building the house, we learned about using tools, being safe on the work site, conducting measurements, using drills, and put up siding. Nothing really surprised me.

However, I learned that instead of getting mad or frustrated, we would just fix anything that need to be fixed. I would say that everybody was kind of nervous when the program first started, but we have learned to get along. Most importantly, now we have become good friends.

Tat O., one of the authors, working with tools for the house

Kevin Sims, one of the authors, working on the beams of the house

We are Bull City YouthBuild: A Collective Blueprint and Collaborative Poem

We are Bull City YouthBuild.

In this final piece of the book, the authors came together to create a collaborative piece entitled, "We are Bull City YouthBuild." This piece represents their collective blueprint---the collective narrative of their experience.

Authors and Teachers of the *Blueprints: Rebuilding Lives and Redesigning Futures*

We are Bull City YouthBuild

Jermaine Quick Jr., Kevin Sims, Nysheed McClinton,
Tat O.

We are unique and intelligent youth
Aiming to be successful in all we do
Ain't nothing like a second chance to succeed in life
So you better come and do what you have to do

We work hard from 9 to 5
Studying hard so we can pass our test
To get our high school diploma
Our hard work pays off when we are sitting at a desk

We will strive for a lifetime of greatness
Thus, we learn from OSHA how to protect ourselves
The worksite is busy and being safe is the key
Using tools correctly is the best way to be

To get a construction trade and never settle for less
We got to do our best to pass our HBI test
We install the cabinets and windows
Doors and HVAC
To make a home for a family to sleep

You will see us moving toward our dreams
Not facing back, pushing forward
Keeping our lives on track
Staying motivated
And keeping in tact
Watch our scene and sit back
And let us do our thing

Author Biographies

Tat O.

Tat O., formerly known as Tatianna Osborne, was born and raised in Durham NC. She was born on May 24, 2000, and is a Gemini, smart, and loves to write and draw. This would be the first book she has ever written.

She is currently 17 years old and was raised by her aunt. Her aunt has 4 kids who she now calls her sister and brothers because she has been with them since I was 3 years old. Her lifetime goal is to be successful in life and own 2 of her own barbershops.

Author Biographies

Nysheed McClinton

Nysheed McClinton is 17 years old and he stays with his mom in Durham, North Carolina. Nysheed started YouthBuild in September 2017 and is looking forward to finishing on January 25, 2018. Nysheed loves playing basketball and football. He finds the staff and students at YouthBuild enjoyable, and has appreciated the relationships he has made. This is Nysheed's first ever published book.

Author Biographies

J'nasi Little

J'nasi Little was born and raised in Durham, NC. He is very outgoing and can rap and sing. He wants to be his own boss and own his own business. He has three siblings who are smart and intelligent in different wants. He always wanted to be write a book, and now he has.

Author Biographies

Jane Rodriguez*

Jane is 16 years old and was raised in Durham, North Carolina. She enjoys spending time with her loved ones. Jane Rodriguez started in YouthBuild on September 2017 and will be graduating on January 25, 2018. She will be attending college in the spring of 2018, and plans to study Architectural Designs. This is Jane's first published book.

*Pseudonym used

Author Biographies

Kevin Sims

Kevin Sims is 25 years old and stays in Durham, North Carolina. He has been with Bull City YouthBuild since March 2017. He has one sister who is 27 years old and they like to make each other laugh. Kevin also likes to listen to music and to play basketball and football. After graduating, he looks forward to owning his own bike shop and doing some driving on the side for income. This will be Kevin's first published book.

Author Biographies

Jermaine Quick Jr.

Jermaine Quick was born and raised in Durham, NC. He is 19 years old and has three siblings. He loves playing the game and can also draw. He wants to be a producer in music and also a secret server in the army. Jermaine is a very creative person and this will be the first book he has ever written.

Blueprints of the Habitat for Humanity House

These sketches are examples of the exterior and sectional blueprints of the house the Bull City YouthBuild students constructed while publishing this book. The interior blueprints of the house are overlaid on the cover of this publication.

Used with permission from Joe Hall,
Construction Instructor

Blueprints of the Habitat for Humanity House

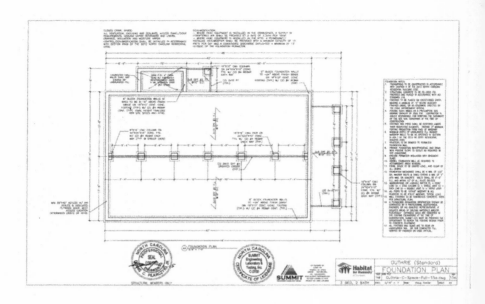

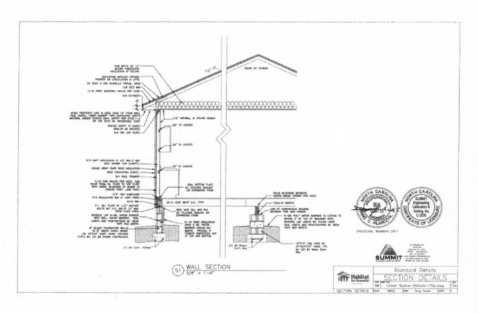

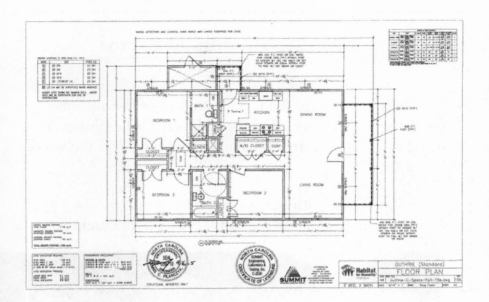

GUTHRIE (Standard)
FLOOR PLAN

3 BED, 2 BATH

Bull City YouthBuild Photos

These photos are the representation of the authors' year together as they achieved their high school diploma and constructed the house from the summer of 2017 to the winter of 2017.

Used with permission from students and
Bull City YouthBuild Directors and Teachers

Teamwork in Summer 2017

Learning with tools and constructing the house in Summer 2017

Bull City YouthBuild Director, Cory Rawlinson, taking a break with the students.

Tat O.'s artwork that was installed on house's air vents at the completion of the project

Examining the interior with Mr. Joe Hall

The finished product: From blueprint to construction
Durham, North Carolina

BUILD YOUR COMMUNITY.

CHANGE YOUR LIFE.

What is YouthBuild?

YouthBuild is an international program funded through grants from the Department of Labor which works with low-income youth to help rebuild their communities and their lives. There are more than 225 YouthBuild programs in the U.S. that have participated in building 17,000 units of affordable housing.

YouthBuild addresses several of the core issues facing low-income communities such as: education, housing, employment, and leadership development. YouthBuild attempts to build a productive future for young men and women who have dropped out of school. The program hopes to attain this goal by providing a way for students to simultaneously serve their communities.

The several programs inside of YouthBuild are:

- Community Service
- Alternative Education
- Job Training/Pre-Apprenticeship
- Leadership Development

Our Program:

Bull City YouthBuild is a full-time, 9-month program that helps you earn your high school equivalency/diploma while giving you hands-on job skills training in the construction industry.

Through the YouthBuild program, our participants will work in the classroom to earn their high school equivalency/diploma while constructing low-income housing through our partnership with Habitat for Humanity of Durham. Participants will have the opportunity to develop leadership skills, build lasting friendships, access career counseling and job or education placement, and earn a construction certificate that will make them highly employable.

Bull City YouthBuild participants can earn up to $200/month while attending the program, and all Bull City YouthBuild graduates will receive a laptop upon completion of the program. More importantly, YouthBuild offers hope and a second chance to overcome obstacles that many of our participants have faced, including poverty, violence, abuse, drugs, fear, and lack of support. Participants will get support from expert staff to help them succeed in the classroom, at the worksite, and in life.

Visit http://www.triangleliteracy.org/bullcityyouthbuild/ for more information.

Triangle Literacy Council

The Triangle Literacy Council's mission is to improve the lives of adults, youth, and families by teaching basic literacy and life skills for economic and social success. For over 47 years, we have served a broad spectrum of individuals including youth (ages 6-16) involved with the juvenile justice system, foster children, unemployed adults, inmates in county jails, digitally-excluded populations, English as a Second language learners, and parents and their young children. We work to ensure that every adult and child in the Triangle is given the opportunity to learn basic skills to help them graduate from high school, earn their GED, or advance in the workplace, and build a better future for themselves and their family. TLC also serves as an NC Works job center to help unemployed adults find and secure jobs. The Bull City YouthBuild program began in 2017 and works with young adults age 16 to 24 in Durham, North Carolina. All of our services are provided at no cost to our students.

About NC STATE College of Education

The college is at the nexus of two high-tech hubs: NC State, a preeminent research university with elite science, technology and math programs; and Raleigh, a cradle of the next wave of tech entrepreneurship.

In that cutting-edge context, the College of Education offers graduate and undergraduate students a personalized experience that equips them for the ever-changing 21st-century classroom. Small classes, cohesive student cohorts and a tight focus on applying research make us a national leader in student success. Visit https://ced.ncsu.edu/about-us/ for more information.

NC STATE UNIVERSITY

Department of
Teacher Education and Learning Sciences

We articulate our vision through our commitment to:

- Developing highly effective teachers in our disciplines through undergraduate and graduate teacher education.
- Inspiring culturally competent educators who are committed to equity and social justice.
- Advancing digital technologies into the professional preparation of teachers and other education professionals.
- Changing the field of education by engaging in research that addresses current challenges.
- Discovering, disseminating and producing new knowledge in our disciplines.